The Outcast Will Outlast

Brandon Griffin

CONTENTS

ACKNOWLEDGMENTS

First and foremost, I want to give God the honor and glory for all of the blessings he has bestowed upon my life; without him there is no me. Thanks for giving me another chance at life to share my story with the world for your glory eternally grateful.

To my Pastor Empress Bolton/ Nathaniel Bolton of Oneway International Ministries: I want to thank God for sending me to the store front church to be restored, revived, renewed, and poured into for such a time as this! I love you and thank you for your sound doctrine, rebukes, and love for me! I appreciate the God in you guys you guys will forever hold a special place in my heart.

To my mentor Tiauna Ross (Coach T) and Miss Benton Harbor 2001: I have so much to say, but what's understood doesn't need to be explained. I thank you for all your mentoring through some of the toughest seasons of my life, especially concerning my book! I love you and thank God we crossed paths in this life.

To my parents: I love you dearly! I appreciate you giving me life.

To my friends: I love you all; thanks for all your support!

To my supporters on Facebook: I appreciate you guys for always believing in the God within me. I thank all of you from the bottom of my heart!

To my prayer group: I thank God for the iron sharpens iron crew. I love you to life!

To the Outcasts: I love you guys and I pray my book has touched you in a special way!

To my late grandmother and grandfather Marshall Lee and Dorothy Bailey: I love and miss you both. Thank you for loving me. I am so grateful for the years God allowed me to be with you. I most definitely will hold our memories in my heart forever.

CHAPTER 1: THE OUTCAST

Psalms 36:9 - "For with you is the fountain of life; in your light we see light."

What is an outcast? This is a good question for me to answer right at the beginning of this book. An outcast is a person who has been rejected by society or a social group. When I look back over my life, I can see there was something different about me that made me "stand out" from everyone else in the world. You are probably wondering what I mean by different. When I think of when God created me, I like to believe he used a special clay to create a uniqueness that would set me apart from everyone else around me. By its definition, uniqueness means being one of a kind; unlike anyone or anything else.

I didn't always see it this way, but God set apart the best for last. It wasn't an easy task to be different because there was so much pressure, adversity, labeling, judgement, cruelty, loneliness, hatred, and peer pressure that came along with the role of being an outcast. A young outcast will often believe there is something wrong with him, but as he ages and grows more confident in who he is, he will adapt. He may think perhaps there is not something wrong with him, but rather something wrong with everyone else.

When you don't know that you are simply being who you were created to be, it can be extremely frustrating trying to fit in with people who are not your kind and are not attached to your destiny. As an outcast, you may fail to see that rejection is for God's protection; it is all part of His plan to keep you protected. Sometimes being different will cause you to be misunderstood when you really mean well. It is hard to explain and express yourself to people around you, especially if they are all the same…like a cult!

Brandon, what does that mean? Let me explain; the definition of cult that I am thinking of is a person or thing that is popular or fashionable, especially among a specific group in society. As an outcast, you are the complete opposite of this.

Thinking back on my early teenage years, I used to dress out of the box, meaning I would wear something that was off the wall or weird to others. From my own perspective, I knew I was the only person who could pull it off. People would often stare at me without saying anything. I felt they were judging me because I was different. Earlier on, I did not understand why I was created to be unique. While looking back over my life, I now understand that being an outcast is not bad. I was born this way! I understand now that I was born to lead and make a bold statement for others to follow their own sense of fashion. This boldness led to me being an outcast because I would dare to be different.

You weren't created to fit into a circle; you were created to be the circle. I'd become frustrated that people wouldn't accept or respect me for who I was. I had to leap over their judgments and be myself, despite how other people responded to me. Sometimes a person's judgment about you is not personal, it's just they don't know who they are yet. Sometimes they can't see that who they are rejecting today may be the very person to help them in life later on. Initially, being the outcast made me feel like I was living out a curse. I had to gain an understanding over time that being the outcast was not a bad thing. I'll tell you more about the outcast in the chapters to come.

As you read beyond this point, you may find yourself in one of these chapters as an outcast. Being different is not something to be ashamed of, but something to be proud of. You were placed on this earth to make a difference and set a standard for generations to come; many of them will be just like you. Creating your own way in the world we live in is a part of what being an outcast is about!

Frustration is part of the preparation. Don't allow your emotions of being set apart take you back to a place called stuck; it will eventually work out in your favor.

CHAPTER 2: IDENTITY ISSUES

Proverbs 15:1 ESV – "A soft answer turns away wrath, but a harsh word stirs up anger."

As far back as I can remember, I'd always struggled with identity issues. Yes, I had a date of birth, a social security number, and a hospital record of whom they said I was, but when I was brought home from the hospital, I was unidentifiable.

Identity and self-esteem problems (what I consider symptoms) were rooted in insecurities and word curses that were spoken throughout my life growing up. These issues caused me to believe something that wasn't true about my life. I didn't plant any seeds of discord during my childhood stages, but the fight was always on. I was tired of always walking around in either defeat or beast mode, ready at any time to defend who I was against people who called me something different from what God had chosen me to be. I'd become a walking time bomb, ready to explode at any sign of a threat.

I was called names like faggot, sissy, punk, gay, weird, crazy, fat, and ugly. These words stirred an angry spirit within me. When I finally clapped back, people probably thought I was crazy. I wasn't crazy. If they only knew what I had gone through behind closed doors. If only they could understand how my innocence was stolen from me at the age of six, causing an identity crisis in my life; maybe then they would watch those words they planted in my life!

Just like me, there are many other people whose identities as people in society today were stolen from them as a result of mixed signals and word curses people have spoken over them as a child. Phrases like You'll never be anything or You're just like your dad. Do you know how planting these types of seeds in someone can scar them for life? Thank God man is not my judge; I would've been in hell already if it wasn't for God and His mercy.

When I was in high school, I was picked on because I didn't fit in with everyone else; I was living a homosexual lifestyle that I was not ashamed of. People used to pick on me because I was little and insulted my intelligence. I was short and gay; they did not think I would fight back. It wasn't that I was scared to fight back; I was afraid of what I was capable of doing because of the anger I had from my experiences growing up.

I remember there was one young man who bullied me every day. I had two friends that would walk me home because, truth be told, I was afraid, but I didn't want to fight at the time. I was all for making peace with everyone because I was already battling with trying to fit in and didn't want to do anything that would make me stand out even more. This particular guy made it known that he did not like me. He made all types of threats, spit on me, and told me, "Don't walk home alone, I'm going to beat you to sleep!" I was afraid. I kept asking God, "Why me?" I had no older siblings to look out for me. I knew if he caught up with me, I was on my own.

One day, I was sitting in choir class when I decided I'd had enough. All those names he called me kept running through my mind. I thought about all the times he picked on me. The anger inside of me boiled over that day. I walked out of class without permission and went to the cafeteria where I knew he would be. I saw him go in. I stood face to face with the guy who had been bullying me. Without warning, I hit him. I kept hitting him for all the times he picked on me. I don't even know how we ended up in the counselor's office, but that's where the fight ended. I showed him no mercy!

Although I had won the fight on that day, it left a scar on my life, and I questioned in the back of mind, "Will I have to fight like this forever?" The high school counselor wanted to talk to me, but I didn't want counseling in high school. I wanted to hurt because I felt that the hurt and anger was what allowed me to fight back and defend myself when I had to. I didn't want to deal with the pain.

I was given a reputation by other people before I could establish one for myself. Instead of hearing encouraging words of wisdom and understanding and good things about life and myself as I grew up, I was torn down with words from family members, church people, and my peers at school. I was already bleeding; the words just made the pain even worse. The spirit of low self-esteem and depression became my constant companion in life.

Because of my identity issues, I wrestled with the

thoughts inside my head for so long. No one took the time to teach me the correct way of living life. These identity issues affected my schooling and my relationships. I was unable to build friendships with people who probably would've meant well for me in my life. I created walls and isolated myself from normal people. The devil will use these attacks to keep you from believing in who God has called you to be, and also to keep you from believing there are people capable of showing you love.

Most of the time when you are trying to find yourself and your way in life, you will struggle to identify who you are. It comes from a deep root inside. Nothing outside of you can destroy you unless you allow it to. This also means that nothing outside of you will fix it either. People tend to cover up issues, making us live a life of lies and make-believe. This happens because we are planting over what really needs to be uprooted.

My life didn't change overnight. There was work to do from the inside this time. It didn't happen overnight; it was a continuation of layers that had to come off me. These layers were rooted deeply because I was carrying something that wasn't mine. It was passed down to me (a repeating cycle) that the enemy thought never could be broken. I had to learn that my identity was through Christ, evidence that His hands were on life from a little boy until now because of Jeremiah 1:5. Once I told myself I was going to get my identity back, start speaking life over myself, and be who God called me to be.

Once I began the stages of finding my identity, I was tested over and over again! Don't think the devil was going to allow me to get away that easily! But I had to unlearn what I knew and relearn me all over again.

I rediscovered my identity on December 16, 2016. I'd relocated back to Hattiesburg, MS and was attending Oneway International Ministries, where my big sister at the time, Pastor Empress Bolton, preached a sermon called "From the Root" and shook my core. I walked into church that day, still hurting from my past. I stood with my hands up, worshipping God. Minister Jenkins came and spoke in my ear and said, "God wants to free you from the residue of childhood molestation." I could hear the walls tumble as the tears streamed down my face. Romans 6:6, "For we know that our old self was crucified with him so that the body ruled by sin might be done away with, that we no longer be a slave to sin."

~~~~~~~~~~~~~~~~~~~~~~~~~~~~~~~~~~~~~~~

People who act tough thrive on feeling like they have power over others. They want to be perceived as being in control and often micromanage others or have unreasonable demands. Mentally strong people, however, are interested in controlling themselves rather than the people around them. When you don't know who you are, you attract people who act tough and only want to control you.

I remember when I met a man that had the face of a prince on the outside, but was a monster when he took that mask off. At the time I met him, I was unstable and unsure of myself. I was using anything and everything outside of myself to accept who I was when this slim, tall and handsome man from Houston, TX came along. He was battling the same thing I was battling, so we connected and dated for a while. At first, he was charming and smooth. The mask slipped when we started doing drugs together. We bonded over our bondage to substance abuse. I escaped through cocaine and pills; he escaped through excessive alcohol. When he was drunk, he was verbally abusive and unpredictable. I saw the scariest demon of my life, and it brought back painful memories from my childhood.

My mom experienced this same kind of abuse when I was a child. At first, I was helpless to intervene and watched fearfully as she suffered through her abuse. One Christmas Eve, my sister and I were sleeping upstairs when I woke to the sound of commotion downstairs. My mother pleaded with my stepfather, "Please don't kill me.....you're hurting me....please." My heart raced, and I could feel the anger building up on the inside. My mother endured many instances of abuse in silence. She never talked about it to anyone.

Even as kids, our stepfather would beat us for minor things like eating too much cereal when we were hungry. There is only so much abuse a person can take without fighting back. One day, a fight broke out between them and I could hear my mother being thrown around and crashing into walls and furniture. She cried and begged for my stepfather to stop, but he wouldn't. I listened for a while until the situation worsened. I rushed into my sister's room and requested she hide until I'd tell her to come out. I ran into the kitchen, snatched the white toaster off the counter, grabbed the biggest knife I could find, and stood until he noticed me. I lost control. I threw the toaster and hit him in the head. He stopped attacking my mother. He stood there, stunned. I wanted to stab him, but instead I told my mother to run across the street and yelled for my sister to come down and go with her. I stood there staring at him, knife in hand. I was blinded by anger, and I did not move until the neighbors came and told me to leave the house. He was arrested that day, and my mother never returned to him.

I thought violence was the only way to solve these things because of the trauma I experienced growing up. When I got into this violent relationship and drugs got involved, it was bound to be an explosive conclusion. I wasn't going to be beaten without fighting back; the hits and fights grew stronger and more dangerous. It all came crashing down with the last fight between us. We were at his house, and he was laying in the bed. I was tired of this relationship; neither one of us were good for each other. I confronted him for cheating and was really trying to get out of the relationship. I told him, "I'm leaving you, I'm done with this." He got out of bed, stood in front of me, and said, "If I can't have you, nobody can." He blocked the door. I felt the same fear and anger I felt the day I fought my stepfather. I pushed him out of the way, and that's when the physical fight broke out. I fought my way out of that apartment and ran for my life. And like my mother did when she escaped, I never looked back from that day forward.

~~~~~~~~~~~~~~~~~~~~~~~~~~~~~~~~~~~

As I stood at the altar that day in December 2016, that little boy inside of me, the scared and angry boy who fought back when he was backed into a corner, cried out and broke free.

As I laid there, Pastor Bolton said to me, "After this day you won't deal with this again. It breaks today!" Even now, I still feel chills through my body, just as it did when she touched me and told me God was giving me my identity back. I have never been the same since that day.

This deliverance process was long, but I didn't give up; no matter what I faced, I kept going.

CHAPTER 3: THE CRY

"Crying is alright in its way while it lasts,
But you have to stop sooner or later
and then still have to decide what to do."
- Author Unknown

When I was young, people thought I was crazy. At school, I was the class clown, always trying to make people laugh and fit in. I would go from laughing to beast mode in seconds, as soon as people pushed my triggers. I started to think something was wrong with me. "What did I do?" Whether I was laughing or fighting, I was constantly questioning whether it was meant for me to be alive. I dealt with this spirit of suicide for years.

On the outside, I was fighting, but on the inside, I was crying. Anger can also be a substitute for emotion. By this I mean that sometimes people make themselves angry so they don't have to feel pain. Anger is an easier emotion than sadness and pain because you can focus anger outside of yourself.

I felt like an outsider; both in my family and around my

classmates at school. I knew who my father was, but he was absent from my life. We lived in the same town, but I only saw him passing by in the street at my grandmother's house or when there was a death in the family. He wasn't connected to me. My mother was sixteen when I was born, and my father, for whatever reason, did not believe I was his child at first. I later discovered that I have fourteen siblings on my father's side; many of them I don't have a relationship with. He had a drug addiction as well, but none of this mattered to me as a child. I just knew he wasn't there for me, and I felt rejected from being left out.

When I was fourteen, my father and I had a conversation that I will never forget. I was at my grandmother's house, sitting on the front porch. My father was walking down the street. He stopped walking and approached me. He said, "Word on the street is that you're gay." I was taken aback. I responded with one question, "Where were you when I was a kid?" He looked shocked that I answered his question this way. He didn't have anything else to say, so he said, "I love you, Son, and I will see you at your grandma's house." He walked away. This was the first and last conversation we had about me being gay.

Even though my dad didn't come around when I was young, I did have my dad's brother, Uncle Shinnara, who was a father figure to me. He would come by every weekend with toys and say to me, "Even though your dad's not here, I'm here." He would spend time with me and always stopped by to check on me whenever he was on my side of town.

I remember being at my aunt's house one Saturday morning. I was excited because I was expecting to see

Uncle Shinnara later that day at my granny's house. My mom came to pick us up earlier than normal. Her white car pulled into the driveway and we got inside. That's when my mom told me that my uncle had been killed. I cried. I couldn't believe it. Uncle Shinnara was the only father figure I had, and on October 29, 1994, he was gunned down and murdered. I was 8-years-old.

When I got to my granny's house, I saw the hurt and anger on her face; this made me even more angry and sad. I suffered from depression for a long time after this.

My daddy was listening to his Tupac and drinking his beer. He cried. I had never seen my dad cry like he did that day. I remember giving him a hug and he said to me, "I love you, Son." My father told me he loved me, but it was my Uncle Shinnara who showed me love through his actions.

My uncle's untimely death left a gap in my life that no one else in the family could fill. So many people pre-judged me on the outside but didn't know I was struggling on the inside. I was bleeding for attention, crying for help, and trying to understand this trial I was walking through. Less attention at home drove me to find love in other places; I became emotionally attached to anybody who gave me attention. That's a whole other book! The one place I found safety in was at church.

I can reflect on a situation that tested me. It was the 3rd Sunday in 2005. I'd arrived at church really needing a word from the Lord that day. My uncle was giving my grandmother a hard time, and they were arguing. I walked to church that morning; the whole time I kept thinking, "I need to get to church, I just need to get to church." When I opened the doors of the church, I was met with stares, laughs, and disapproving looks on the faces of my fellow church members.

As I approached my seat, I was asked by the assistant to meet my pastor in the pastor's studies for a quick meeting. When I closed the door behind me, the pastor asked me to sit. At this point, I was prepared for the worst. I sat in his office. "It was brought to my attention that you were trying to touch a young man on the bus after Bible Study Youth Night on Wednesday."

I was shocked and quickly said, "No, that's not true."

"I also was told that you said my sons were gay."

I was so confused. I didn't know anything about the rumor of his sons being gay and I certainly didn't say anything like it! I considered his sons as my little brothers and the pastor and his wife as my spiritual parents. I looked up to them as role models. I would have never said anything like this about them. I was thinking to myself, "If they know my spirit, they should know me better than to believe something like this. As far as the rumor about the young man on the bus, what really took place was different from the story he'd been told.

After service on Wednesday, I had been on my way home on the church bus when the young man sitting next to me passed me a note. This was unusual, but I opened the note and read it: "Brandon, I want to be gay, or at least try it. What do you recommend?" I replied to him directly by saying, "No you do not, man. Live your life for God because this is a battle that is hard to get free from. Don't try it!" Before the bus stopped at his destination, he started to touch my leg. I removed his hand and said, "Stop! That is not how you do things. You can't invite yourself to touch someone." The church bus driver was looking in the rear view mirror, and I was so shocked this young man had done this knowing the driver could see him. What I did not know was that the young man got off the bus in anger and was intent on doing something that would hurt me to the core. I was trying to encourage the young man not to engage in these types of sexual sins because it is not easy to get free from. I never expected him and the bus driver to assassinate my character and tell a lie when I was trying to do the right thing.

Before I could tell the pastor what really happened that day on the bus, I was hit with these words: "You are not allowed to attend this church anymore." I tried to explain. I said, "I have a note to prove I did not do this," but he was already done talking to me. I was asked to leave God's house and never come back. I was hurt and angry and I left before I acted out on how I felt. I dropped my head and wept. When I reached the parking lot, one of the sisters at the church asked me to come back inside and attend service. She may not have known what was going on. "F*** the church" was the bitter response that came out of my mouth. The rejection hit me harder when it came from a place that I thought would change me and heal me. Unfortunately, I decided to return to the same lifestyle I was trying to get free from.

Let me clarify this. My first response to being rejected at the church was to immediately go back to what was comfortable. Sometimes we can find ourselves waiting to be rejected again so we can go back to Satan's games or his web of deceit. I wasn't strong in standing in Christ and resisting the devil. The incident at the church opened a wound in my heart that was not completely healed. I was trying to break free from the hurt of being excluded from church. This situation gave me a different perspective about the house of God.

I found comfort in hanging with my gay friends and using drugs and alcohol. My friends were like family to me, yet I still couldn't get my mind off what happened. I felt like I was an outsider, even in the house of God, and it made me angry with God as well! I would say things like, "How could you allow this to happen, God?" or "Why me?" I often asked those questions when I was alone with God. Even though I was angry, no matter what, I never stopped praying, because I knew that God was my only hope of getting my life straightened out.

Months had gone by since that incident occurred at the church; I was still not going to any churches. I would see various members from my former church. They would ask me, "Are you okay?" I always replied with, "All is well," even though I knew good and well that all was not well. I'd decided that I didn't want them to see me hurting. It was a way to protect myself and also a way for me to speak about what I wanted to happen in my life. One particular day I ran into one of my big sisters whom I truly admired. She stopped me in my tracks as I was leaving the corner store. I was high on drugs and was buying cigarillos to smoke.

"The pastor and first lady have been asking about you," she said. I responded, "I'm never coming back to church!" She hugged me so tight and began to minister to me and encourage me. Even though I was trying to hold up a hard exterior while she was ministering to me, I broke down and told her how I felt. I told her the incident at the church almost drove me to take my own life. She shared what the pastor said to her, "If you see Brandon, tell him I love him." I said to her, "I am not ready to forgive just yet." She invited me to come back to church, but I did not accept the offer. Later that week, my grandmother told me that the pastor had come by the house looking for me. I told my granny that I didn't want to see anyone from the church.

I did not know that my grandmother had sat with the pastor when he stopped by and showed him the letter the young man gave me on the bus. She talked to him while I was in the backyard hiding and smoking my weed. He stopped by to tell me he was concerned about me and to give him a call. I still did not want to go to church. It was too much of an embarrassment for me to go back there.

The following Saturday, I ran into another brother from the church. He said, "The Pastor told the whole congregation to tell me to come to church that Sunday. He really wants to see you." Something inside of me broke through the wall I'd kept up all this time. "I'll be there," I said.

I walked into the church that Sunday, treading lightly. I was determined to walk in with my head held high in the air. I did not want anyone to see me the same way they saw me the last time I was there. I was unsure and did not trust anyone. I sat all the way in the back; I'd gotten high before I came there. The pastor called me to the front of the church. I walked carefully with a startled look on my face as I approached the altar. On the inside, I felt convicted.

The pastor stood there, in front of everyone, with the first lady at his side. "Brandon, I've been worried about you. God would not let me sleep for two weeks after that happened because I was worried about your soul and my conscience wouldn't let me rest." He continued with everyone, including my accuser, watching. "I'm sorry for what happened. I want to apologize for how I handle things. Will you forgive me?"

I broke down and cried. I prayed so many nights about this, and even though I'd gone my own way, God answered my prayers. I hugged my leaders and apologized for what I said in my anger. Everyone welcomed me back into the church. I appreciated that they dealt with the apology publicly considering my humiliation had been public. But although I had re-entered the church, I still had another wound that would take time to fully heal.

CHAPTER 4: I HAVE A SECRET

Deuteronomy 31:8: "The LORD himself goes before you and will be with you; he will never leave you nor forsake you. Do not be afraid; do not be discouraged."

I had a drug dependency that I kept a secret. I kept this secret to protect myself. I thought I was doing the right thing, and in a twisted way, I felt justified. The toxic experiences I went through in life were difficult to deal with on a daily basis. At first, drugs helped me escape some of the pain, but it eventually made matters worse. I went from having a secret to having an addiction.

Addiction is a complicated condition. People who suffer from addiction have an intense focus on drugs to the point that it takes over their life. They use alcohol or drugs even when they know it will cause problems. Several effective treatments are available to help people recover from addiction and lead normal, productive lives. These treatments include options like halfway houses, counseling, therapy, or having an accountability partner. People may desire to stop doing something that is not good for them; but sometimes, if it is a stronghold, they will struggle to stop the addictive cycle. I was one of these people. I knew drugs were not good for me; yet I struggled to break free from it. It was a stronghold that would not let me go without a fight.

Never in a million years did I think I would do drugs. I grew up watching my family members use drugs and sex as a part of their regular routines and I vowed I would never use them myself. But there was already a sinister plan to keep these toxic behaviors in our family from generation to generation. I knew I was going to be different. I did not count on the fact that strongholds are real. Not everyone takes the path of drug abuse, but for some it can be a familiar path toward dealing with issues or avoiding them altogether. I encourage anyone who is struggling with drug abuse to get the help they need. I kept my addiction a secret until I couldn't hold it anymore. It would have been better for me to get help before it went too far.

I started out smoking marijuana. As time went on, I was introduced to cocaine. I went from using cocaine as a party drug to adopting it as a lifestyle. I would go from doing a little bit to doing 8-balls; I stayed up all night getting high, reading my Bible and masturbating uncontrollably. I consider these things as signs of death knocking on my door, but I thank God he didn't take my mind. The devil will do all he can to kill you before the breakthrough. In my case, he couldn't destroy me completely because God still had his hands on me! I was still going to church, shouting, dancing, speaking in tongues, but I was addicted to cocaine. I would go to parties to have my party favorites. The gay lifestyle I was living was no fun without the party packs! When I was high I felt like I was at peace, but it was a false sense of peace. I had no worries until I started thinking about my past. I was in a dark place in my life, and instead of going up like Christians are supposed to, I was going backwards.

I would cry out sometimes, "God, please take the taste of cocaine out of my mouth!" But I did not give up cocaine as a coping mechanism. Whenever I was upset, I would get high. The angrier I got, the higher I would get. Cocaine was a viable to way to escape without having constant thoughts of suicide. I even told myself that cocaine saved my life because I was getting high instead of committing suicide!

In reality, cocaine didn't help me. It negatively affected my mental health, my body, my money, and I was losing myself. There is no doubt about it; I was an addict. Instead of buying food, I bought drugs. Sometimes when I ran out of money I would sleep with the dope man in Houston. I was broken and couldn't afford it, but I needed it. I would call my dope man back to back, at all times of the day and night, because what once was a party drug was now completely taking over my life. I remember thinking to myself, "Where did I go wrong?" I was losing weight and didn't have an appetite for food. I was mad and anxious when I didn't have any drugs to use. I remember one time I'd gotten so high my anxiety had me outside walking around my apartment complex to calm my body down. I am sure I looked crazy to anybody looking at me that day. That was what cocaine was doing to me. I felt like it was destroying my heart beat! The enemy of my soul wanted to destroy me before I could get back to God. I would always pray before going to sleep, "God, please don't take me out like this."

I couldn't keep this secret in my life forever. On May 28, 2017, I was celebrating my best friend's birthday party. The drugs were there, but I had gotten tired of wearing a mask. I knew I was heading down a road that would lead to my destruction eventually. All I heard in my head was the wages of sin is death. I was getting ready to take a bump when I heard a loud voice in my ear say, "Put it down and don't touch it again." I knew this was the voice of God warning me one last time. I couldn't do it. I went to flush the drugs down the toilet and I never looked back!

See, the devil will have you doing wrong and thinking that your grace won't run out. I thought cocaine was what I needed to escape the pressures of life, not realizing that the thing about a diamond is that it has to go through the fire in order to shine! I was trying to shortcut the process of becoming. It felt good to release myself from the generational curse that was passed down to me and finally break the cycle. Now that I'm free, some of my close family members are also off drugs. It was a long process. I had to seek God and erase every person out of my life that did drugs. I deleted the drug dealer's number and stopped going to parties. The last time I talked to my drug dealer I said to him, "This will be my last time calling you. I'm quitting and I'm going to delete your number." He responded by saying, "That's good. You don't need drugs where you are going in life."

I withdrew from people and places I used to be around. I spent the first six months fighting against the urge to use drugs. I spent another six months away from triggers. I shut down all outside influences. Having said that, the healing process on the inside was the toughest part of my walk. I started using spiritual meditation and prayer as a way to deal with my issues. To fall asleep, I would listen to gospel music and prayer at night to keep my heart from racing. Sometimes when you withdraw from heavy drug use, your body and mind will try to convince you that you need it; that something will go wrong with you unless you use it. I knew that wasn't the truth, so I fought with my mind and body by strengthening my soul and spirit through building a stronger connection with God.

Two weeks after I quit, I started going through problems in my body. One night, I was getting ready to go to bed when a strange event occurred. I'd left something downstairs and I tried to hurry down to get it. I'm not sure if I missed a step, but I fell down the flight of stairs and hurt myself badly. I had a swollen lip and a missing tooth! I went to the hospital where they ran multiple tests on me. They prescribed me an inhaler and pain medications and sent me home. From there, I had more issues. I developed a cough; the coughing became so bad that I began to have seizures. I went to the hospital multiple times. They could not identify any root causes. My heart and other organs were healthy; the testing never yielded any specific issues. Yet I was still having all of these strange symptoms.

Another issue sent me back to the emergency room. It was a Saturday night and I was at my aunt's house getting ready for church. I'd fallen asleep on the couch. The next thing I remember is waking up on the floor with blood gushing from the side of my head. Apparently, I'd fallen off the couch in my sleep. My aunt took me back to the hospital. When they ran tests, the doctors referred me to a cardiologist because they believed I had an enlarged heart.

I followed up with the cardiologist on the following Tuesday. The cardiologist conducted more testing to monitor my heart. When the test results came back, I did not have an enlarged heart. The cardiologist was as shocked as I was that my results came back with a good report. They sent me home with a monitoring device to wear for the next two weeks. No problems were found. They also did an echogram and the results showed no issues with my heart.

As I was going through this entire process, I leaned on the following scripture: Psalm 51:10 KJV "Create in me a clean heart, O God; and renew a right spirit within me." I knew I had to release some unforgiveness I was not dealing with from my past. My relationship with my mother was strained at that time. When she reached out to me to talk, I was open and willing to reconnect in a way that I hadn't been before. I found myself forgiving and letting go of a lot of things that happened in my past. I did not have any other symptoms of heart problems or problems with seizures after I released the unforgiveness I had in my heart.

There were times when I thought I wasn't going to make it along this journey, yet I'm writing this book today because God wasn't through with me on earth yet. I still had work to do. I was built to OUTLAST!

CHAPTER 5: THE TURNAROUND

Exodus 15:26, "For I am the Lord who heals you."

During my mid teenage years, I searched for love and began having relationships with men. The seeds that were sown into me over my life began to manifest. I was introduced to the spirit of homosexuality at the age of six, when I was molested by one of my younger cousins. If that were not enough, I was later sexually assaulted by a person who everyone around me thought could be trusted as a caretaker. This man took my innocence away from me. Many nights I slept with the covers over my head in fear that it would happen again. Unfortunately for me, the abuse happened repeatedly; over and over again. I used to be the type of person to keep everything in and go on with my life. I never understood why I had to go through all of this in my childhood. Everything around me was toxic.

I felt I couldn't get love at home. I was determined to find love on my own because all I wanted was to be loved. I used money and resources to earn love and friendships with people, but what they say is true: money couldn't buy me love. I did not feel that I was worth loving without having something to offer. Later on, these same friends and love interests would abandon me because of what they heard about me; some of them judged me by my outer appearance.

I tried to date girls, but it wouldn't last long because I didn't look like a regular boy. One day, I tested the spirit of homosexuality even though I was nervous to. I was taught in church that it was a sin. I knew it was a sin, but I was crying out from the little boy that was molested and touched. Everyone else around me was so toxic with their own drugs, drinking, partying, and secret lifestyles. No one took the time to even notice I was hurting, injured, and abused. I turned to other things for healing instead of turning to God. See, the enemy knows how to play tricks; he has many clever devices. He knew I was called but did not want me to know I was called. I felt nasty; I would take long showers and I sit and cry as I remembered the night my innocence was taken from me.

My abuser always made sure everyone else was asleep. I would tremble in fear when I heard his footsteps approaching me. I would feel his hands rubbing on my thighs and gripping my waist as he said sweet nothings in my ear. I would lie still and try to be asleep or take my mind somewhere else, somewhere other than that room. He would finish his business with me and go away afterwards. I suffered in silence because I was sure no one would believe me if I told them what was happening to me. As time passed, I knew what to expect and I became numb to being molested by him. The spirit of confusion made me feel like right was wrong and wrong was right.

Even when I would be at school, other young boys would look at my body. When we made eye contact, I already knew what that spirit was. I remained silent.

Back in those days, there was a black gay site called "BGC" where straight, bisexual, and gay guys met to hook up for one night stands or relationships. As I grew older, the spirit of homosexuality was deeply rooted in me. I looked to older men for the love and affection I was missing in my life. I still went to church. At that time, my pastor and first lady had taken me in when I left my family church. They taught me to know God in a non-transitional realm. Even though they taught me the truth and gave sound instruction, they didn't know I had baggage that came with me. I was a young guy seeking help and living a risky lifestyle. I lied to men about my age. I lied to men to get things I wanted. I would meet with men to have sex with them. I felt my body was changing and getting sicker.

One night, I met a guy from Wisconsin who was in his mid-thirties. I'd met him on the chat line and we entered a relationship. I even moved to Wisconsin to be with this man. I'd discovered over the course of our relationship that he was HIV positive. We never had sex with each other, something wouldn't let me do it. The crazy thing about this is that I also believed I had HIV, although I did not get tested to confirm it. I was scared because of the mistakes I had made dealing with men in the past. When my relationship with him ended, I moved back to Benton Harbor, MI; back to my grandmother's house. I was sad about the loss of this relationship. I was still vulnerable and wanted to be loved by someone.

I felt sick and nothing had improved. I did not get tested, even though I knew I was not well. One day, I went to church and I met an anointed man of God named Alex. He took me under his wings, mentored me, and helped me in a godly way. I didn't know what a prophet was until I joined Greater Community COGIC where my leaders and spiritual parents were Lady Trina Wells and Nathaniel Wells. Looking back on this experience, I now believe that Alex was a prophet.

On January 29, 2006, Alex called me to his house for a deliverance service. Let's start with the definition of scared: feeling fear or apprehension. Scared means being in a state of fear, nervousness, or panic. I was scared to open to people because of being an outcast. I suffered from this sickness but didn't know God had a plan for my life!

He laid hands on me, told me to put on a white shirt, and got a bucket so I could purge the sickness "God is about to heal your body from every infirmary." I didn't know what to say: he called out that sickness, healed me, and told me I that when I'd go back to the clinic to get retested, they wouldn't find nothing. Him and his girlfriend prayed over me. I coughed up every infection, my past, and sickness in that bucket, and I felt new when I finished purging. I felt a difference in my body, something I'd never experienced! I tried to tell someone, but they didn't believe me. The Bible says not to cast your pearls before swine. You can't share everything with people who don't have a mindset like yours. It is also problematic to share something before it's time.

On February 12, 2006 I went to the health department in my hometown with God, and a lady prayed with me before I got re-tested. My results came back and they were negative. I think they must have been just as surprised as I was because they required me to take another test. When the results came back, they were negative. They tested me one last time. The test came back with the same results: negative! The medical staff confirmed I did not have HIV. I cried and cried. I knew at that moment God healed me.

I went back to Alex to show him my report and proof of God's deliverance and healing. He cried tears of joy and gratitude because he labored for my deliverance and God was being faithful to His word as written in James 5:16 KJV, "Confess your faults one to another, and pray one for another, that ye may be healed. The effectual fervent prayer of a righteous man availeth much." From that day forward God has been the healer in my life!

Sometimes God does impossible things for the ones who are battered, bruised and left for dead. He is the One who can turn your test into a testimony! I knew I had purpose and that God had a plan for me.

CHAPTER 6: THE PURGE

Psalm 57:1, "Cleanse me with hyssop, and I will be clean; wash me, and I will be whiter than snow."

This is the process that is the most important when being delivered; it's a time-consuming process, so I thought I was free once I stopped, but I didn't know I had to undergo the final stages to be totally free.

The process of a purging - In Christianity, deliverance ministry refers to the activity of cleansing a person of demons and evil spirits in order to address problems manifesting in their life as a result of the presence of said entities.

You must purge every unclean spirit and residue that is left after the deliverance to walk in your purpose, ventral full conscious acceptance of your entire self – meaning that you feel at peace with yourself, and love yourself to feel complete, healthy, and whole within. Forgiveness floods the system and enables you to be more compassionate and accepting of others.

I remember a time when I was transitioning to finding a place after being evicted from my apartment; not because I was doing drugs; I didn't want to pay the rent for another month. My lease was almost up. I was disobedient, rebellious, and full of pride because I would rather stick it out rather than go stay with people; all because of the rejection I had already endured but had not fully let go of. So after taking all my money, I stayed at an extended stay motel.

One Sunday morning, I woke at 5:00 am. My stomach was on fire and I purged blue and purple fluid. I wailed for 3 hours straight face-down, and on that down time I had finally released that bitterness and resentment. I knew this was not a medical situation; this was a spiritual situation. Though I was a grown man of 32 years old, I was holding a grudge against my father for not being present in my life. I had a few other personal issues against others that I also had not fully released yet. That Sunday, I finally let it go through the purge. I realized I was mad at my brothers and sisters because my father was in their life and not mine. I had unresolved resentment; now let me tell you what resentment means: bitter indignation at having been treated unfairly.

I wanted to let go but didn't know how. The purge helped me release some brokenness that I had left unresolved. I knew in order to fully operate in life I had to let it go and let it out! I didn't accept the fact that I was already free, but I needed to be delivered. I remember when my first purging came at 5 am prayer at Oneway International Ministries. Every Tuesday was 5 am prayer and I would push myself to get up so I could be there. I was faithful in prayer. While I was on the floor, my pastor came and ushered in the beginning of my deliverance. She broke the drug addiction off my bloodline, and I started to purge blood. It wasn't continuous blood; it was a purging of all the toxic things I put in my body. I felt a breaking I hadn't felt in years! Every service and every day forward, I felt a release. I felt the generational curses being broken off! Indeed, the process was challenging because a purging was for my good! My Pastor preached a message in this particular scripture that stuck with me for the rest of my life. Romans 8:28 NIV: "And we know that in all things God works for the good of those who love him, who have been called according to his purpose." She would always say when it got too tough and hard "Don't stop coming." Purging is a part of the process; in order to be delivered, you must be purged to get to your place of destination!

I also remember another time of purging after recovering from my addiction. I was on fire up early to go to 5 am prayer. At this time, I didn't have a vehicle, so I walked six miles to get there. I was pressing my way because I knew another level of deliverance was about to happen for me. When I made it to the altar, it became a bed to me. I laid on the altar, crying loud, and my spirit and my Pastor heard me!

After I had a spiritual out of body experience, Lady Bolton laid hands on me. As she touched me, she said, "It breaks today! Every soul tie that is not yours is loose; and every habit and general curse is broken today!" I purged real blood for at least 10 minutes. I had a loud wail in my belly that morning; I felt so free! Lady Bolton gave me a white towel and said, "Trust the process."

Before this moment, I mistakenly thought I was completely delivered because I had a good shout or a had a prophecy spoken over my life. Purging is not easy; it's a process. You have to wait on God throughout this process and keep pressing. As Isaiah 40:31 KJV says, "But they that wait upon the Lord shall renew their strength; they shall mount up with wings as eagles; they shall run, and not be weary; and they shall walk, and not faint." I didn't know before this point that my purging had taught me how to forgive, love, and be humble. When you can conquer being purged, you have won the victory over your life!

CHAPTER 7: OUT OF THE FIRE

Ecclesiastes 7:8, "Better is the end of a thing than the beginning thereof."

Now this chapter is the conclusion to the matter of my book. Whew! When I think about the price I had to pay to get to this place! The beginning was the outcast part of my life but the end is the outlasting part. For two months, I went through a dry season where I was in a place called stuck. I didn't receive a prophetic word from anyone. I felt alone. I felt as if nobody cared. I was at my wits end concerning everything in my life. I was angry, confused, and almost left everything to walk away.

Had I done that, everything I stood for would've been in vain. God was sending me signs through text messages from people, prophetic dreams, and encouraging words from others of what was to come! Oh boy. I didn't know it was going to be a quiet period, but it caused me to start dealing with myself. See, sometimes when God tries to deal with you, He brings to you a quiet place where you can deal with yourself. But when He is ready to move, He will send a sign or a message.

The first sign was a message sent to me that read, "Message for you: Don't get too comfortable. You're about to move to a whole different situation altogether. You're about to move to a whole new situation. Can't wait to see what this means for you." On November 10, 2019, I got another message that changed my life forever. I'll never forget the words I read while I sat in church that day: "You are going to come out one way or the other." I thought to myself, 'God is about to move for me,' but what I didn't know was that it was not going to happen the way I thought it would.

It was my mother's 50th birthday party at the family church. After leaving my church, I celebrated this occasion with my family. After leaving the event, I went home to take a nap around 5:30pm. I read my Bible, watched a movie, prayed, and took a nap. I remember waking to smoke around me and the sound of the glass window in my bedroom shattering. Someone had thrown a bottle through the window to wake me up. That was the only sound I heard from being in a deep sleep. I ran outside to a safe distance. When I turned around, I was astounded to see my whole apartment ablaze and on fire! Yes, I ran out and left everything behind. My thoughts became prayers, "Oh Lord, please don't let me lose the little bit that I had left," but I trusted God with the outcome because He'd once again saved my life. They told me they had kicked my door down, broken my apartment windows trying to wake me. They wanted to save me but could not get to me! Yet I was unharmed; I did not even inhale smoke because I came out one way or the other, just like God's messenger told me I would.

Although I was physically unharmed in the fire, I did not come out of that building the same way as I went in. I was changed, almost like a spiritual death and rebirth. I realized now that I had to die in that fire. Let me explain what I mean. 2 Corinthians 5:17: "Therefore, if anyone is in Christ, he is a new creation; old things have passed away; behold, all things have become new."

Because the old ways of doing things could not live in me any longer, the fire was to purify me for a new beginning. I couldn't die a physical death; I had work to do. I outlasted it God gave me the victory over death! The enemy had a plot, but God had a plan.

The word outlast simply means to endure or last longer than. I truly believe that better is the end of a thing than the beginning! After reading the previous chapters about the suffering, molestation, anger, and being the outcast; I want to remind you that I've outlasted everything I've ever gone through.

Sometimes we don't fully understand that in order to get to something you've never had, you need to go through something you've never been through before! My suffering was not in vain! I did a complete turnaround with my life. I became free from drugs, removed the hate from my heart, and forgave people even when they were not sorry. I healed from the past hurt and disappointments of my childhood and recovered from the loss of loved ones.

In order to move my life forward, I enrolled in college in 2017 at American Intercontinental University and received my Associates Degree in Business Administration. Not long after, I purchased my first car, got my joy back, and after years of running from my calling, preached my first real sermon in 2018. I developed an awesome relationship with my family members and became a mentor for young people who were going through some of the same challenges that I went through. Elect Lady Donna Beard told me once before, "Your misery, is your ministry." I finally came to understand what she meant by that. I joined Oneway International Ministry where the awesome leadership pushed me to outlast and believe in my purpose through faith. Pastor Empress Bolton encouraged me to never stop coming; no matter how hard it got I kept going! I did what they said I couldn't do…outlast!

Romans 8:28: "And we know that all things work together for good to those who love God, to those who are called according to His purpose." Remember this: It's not about what you go through; it's about how you go through it. The outcast will OUTLAST!

ABOUT THE AUTHOR

Brandon Griffin is the founder and owner of Outcast Outlasting Designs LLC. Brandon earned an associate degree in Business Administration from American InterContinental University in 2019. He earned a bachelor's degree in Healthcare Management from American Intercontinental University in 2020.

Brandon is a minister, prophet, and mentor to many young people who have faced similar challenges in life. He also serves as the senior leader of his Outreach ministry, the No Judgment, Free Zone.

Brandon enjoys praying for people, cooking, loving his family, and making people laugh. Brandon was also featured on the "Sunday Best" show in 2013 on the BET Network. Brandon is a huge supporter of the Miss Benton Harbor pageant and has served many years as the historian for the organization. You can contact Brandon through the contact information listed below:

Email: brandon.griffin21@yahoo.com
Phone: 601-658-7074
Facebook: Brandon Griffin
Instagram: Outcast_outlast2

Made in the USA
Columbia, SC
16 August 2020

16537654R00026